W9-BXZ-206

Where Words

Above and Below

by Tami Johnson

Capstone
press

Mankato, Minnesota

A+ Books are published by Capstone Press,
151 Good Counsel Drive, P.O. Box 669, Mankato, Minnesota 56002.
www.capstonepress.com

1 2 3 4 5 6 12 11 10 09 08 07

Library of Congress Cataloging-in-Publication Data
Johnson, Tami.
    Above and below / by Tami Johnson.
    p. cm. — (A+ books. Where words)
    Summary: "Simple text and color photographs introduce basic concepts of above
and below"—Provided by publisher.
    Includes bibliographical references and index.
    ISBN-13: 978-0-7368-6735-1 (hardcover)
    ISBN-10: 0-7368-6735-X (hardcover)
    ISBN-13: 978-0-7368-7853-1 (softcover pbk.)
    ISBN-10: 0-7368-7853-X (softcover pbk.)
    1. Orientation—Juvenile literature. I. Title. II. Series.
BF299.O7J64 2007
153.7'52—dc22   2006022806

Credits
Megan Schoeneberger, editor; Juliette Peters, designer; Charlene Deyle, photo researcher;
    Scott Thoms, photo editor

Photo Credits
Capstone Press/Karon Dubke, 21 (foreground)
Corbis/Bill Ross, 29 (bottom); Charles Mauzy, 28 (bottom); Jeffrey L. Rotman, 11; Jim Zuckerman, 12; Kazuyoshi
    Nomachi, 29 (middle); Post-Houserstock/Dave G. Houser, 8; Rudy Sulgan, 14–15; Tom Brakefield, 13
Dwight R. Kuhn, 7
Getty Images Inc./The Image Bank/Gabriel M. Covian, 23; Photographer's Choice/Gail Shumway, cover;
    Photonica/Michelle Pedone, 25; Stone/Stuart O'Sullivan, 26–27; Taxi/Jim Cummins, 24
James P. Rowan, 9
Minden Pictures/Michael Quinton, 10
Shutterstock/ariadna, 19; Brian Erickson, 16; Cary Kalscheuer, 22; Gennady Imeshev, 28 (top); GeoM, 20;
    Michael Hawk, 29 (top); Pathathai, 21 (background); Rainbow, 6; WizData Inc., 17, 18; zastavkin, 4–5

Note to Parents, Teachers, and Librarians
Where Words uses color photographs and a nonfiction format to introduce readers to the vocabulary of space.
Above and Below is designed to be read aloud to a pre-reader, or to be read independently by an early reader.
Images and activities encourage mathematical thinking in early readers and listeners. The book encourages
further learning by including the following sections: Table of Contents, Fun Facts, Glossary, Read More, Internet
Sites, and Index. Early readers may need assistance using these features.

Table of Contents

What Is Above? What Is Below?

Above is higher.
Below is lower.
Clouds are above.
Grass is below.

Birds fly above us.

Worms crawl below us.

Animals Above and Below

An eagle builds its nest
high above the ground.

A prairie dog lives
in a burrow
below the ground.

Black bear cubs climb high above the forest floor to hide.

A dolphin calf swims below its mother
to stay safe in the deep ocean.

Giraffes stretch their long necks to eat leaves that grow high above them.

Anteaters use their long snouts
to find food in the ground below.

Above and Below in the City

Stop! On a traffic light,
the red light is above the
yellow light.

Go! The green light is
below the yellow light.

From above, you can see the cars on the busy street below.

From below, you can see buildings
towering above you.

A monorail carries riders above crowded roads and speeding cars.

A subway train speeds along
tracks below the city.

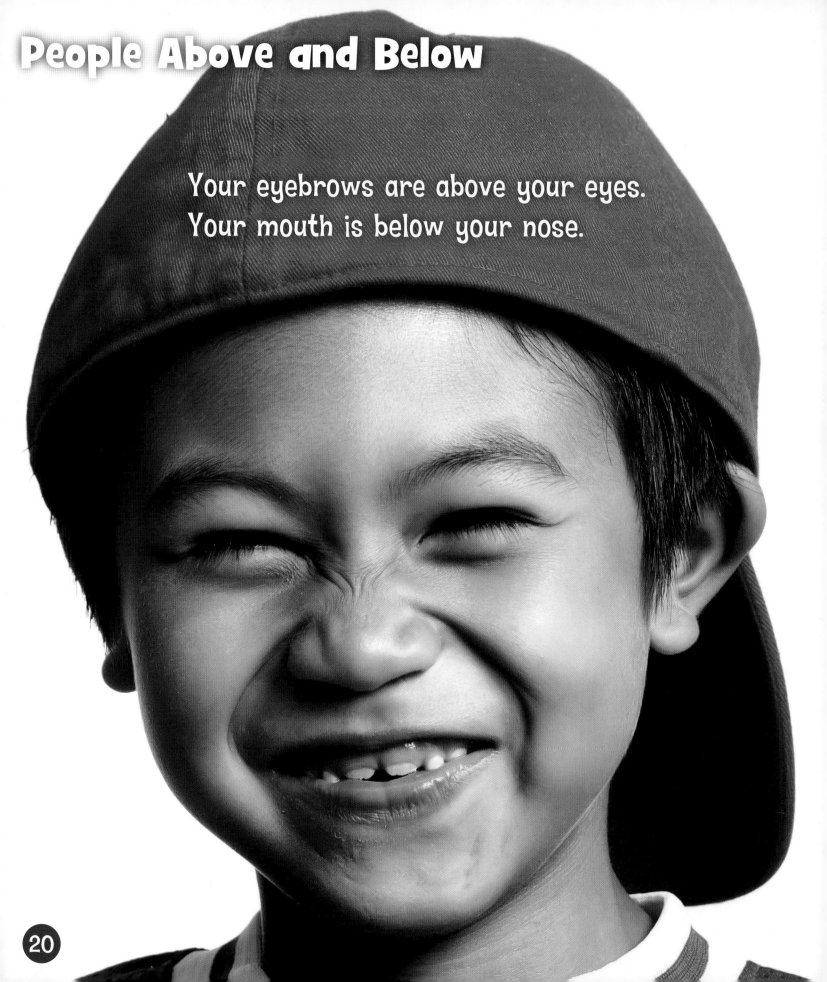

People Above and Below

Your eyebrows are above your eyes.
Your mouth is below your nose.

Your feet are below your ankles.
Your knees are above your ankles.

Some people work high
above the ground.

Some people work
below the ground.

Umbrellas above our heads keep us dry.

Mats below us keep us
safe in case we fall.

Imagine flying through the sky above like a bird. What would you see below?

Above and Below Facts

What does above sea level or below sea level mean? Sea level is a term for the surface of the ocean. We measure the height of mountains and the depth of valleys by comparing them to sea level.

California's Death Valley is 282 feet (86 meters) below sea level. It is the lowest point in the United States.

Alaska's Mount McKinley is 20,320 feet (6,194 meters) above sea level. It is the tallest mountain in North America.

Mount Rushmore in South Dakota rises 5,700 feet (1,737 meters) above sea level. The faces of George Washington, Thomas Jefferson, Theodore Roosevelt, and Abraham Lincoln are carved into the side of this mountain.

Cirrus clouds form 20,000 feet (6,096 meters) above us in the sky. These high clouds usually signal fair weather.

High-speed trains run along the Channel Tunnel. This tunnel is 150 feet (46 meters) below the English Channel between France and England.

Glossary

anteater (ANT-ee-tur)—a South American mammal with a very long tongue and snout that it uses to search for ants and other small insects to eat

burrow (BUR-oh)—a tunnel or hole in the ground made or used by a rabbit, prairie dog, or other animal

cirrus clouds (SIHR-uhss KLOUDZ)—high, thin clouds made of ice crystals that look like strands of white silk

monorail (MON-uh-rayl)—a railroad that runs on one rail, usually high above the ground

prairie dog (PRAIR-ee DAWG)—a small animal that is related to the squirrel

sea level (SEE LEV-uhl)—the average level of the surface of the ocean, used as a starting point from which to measure the height or depth of any place

snout (SNOUT)—the long front part of an animal's head that includes the nose, mouth, and jaws

subway (SUHB-way)—a system of trains that runs underground in a city

Read More

Bertolucci, Cristiano. *Animals Above and Below Water.* Contrasts. Columbus, Ohio: Waterbird Books, 2003.

Redding, Sue. *Up Above and Down Below.* San Francisco: Chronicle Books, 2006.

Rivera, Sheila. *Above and Below.* First Step Nonfiction. Minneapolis: Lerner, 2005.

Internet Sites

FactHound offers a safe, fun way to find Internet sites related to this book. All of the sites on FactHound have been researched by our staff.

Here's how:

1. Visit *www.facthound.com*

2. Choose your grade level.

3. Type in this book ID **073686735X** for age-appropriate sites. You may also browse subjects by clicking on letters, or by clicking on pictures and words.

4. Click on the **Fetch It** button.

FactHound will fetch the best sites for you!

Index